a PENNY is Everything

Luke 21:1-4 FOR CHILDREN

Written by Walter Wangerin Jr.
Illustrated by Jack Glover

ARCH Books

CONCORDIA PUBLISHING HOUSE LTD., LONDON, E. C. 1
MANUFACTURED IN THE UNITED STATES OF AMERICA

ISBN 0-570-06084-2

Concordia Publishing House
St. Louis London

This city is Jerusalem;
It's built on seven holy hills
With crooked valleys in between,
And houses scattered round like pills.

Some houses on some hills are rich:
Three doorways where four horses wait,
Five servants, seven olive trees,
And lights left on till very late.

Some valley shacks are very poor:
One doorway made of sunburnt clay,
One donkey, one brown bramble bush,
And sunlight only in the day.

P. Benjamin Methuselah,
A little boy with a mighty will,
Has one whole bedroom for himself:
His house is on a wealthy hill.

He owns two closets filled with sacks,
Each sack stuffed full of handsome toys,
Each toy (and these, my friend, are facts)
A toy that makes a lot of noise.

But what could someone say of John,
Whose valley shack is down below?
Not much; not much; he has a room—
The one room in the house, you know.

A one-room house, no closet space,
No place to keep a lot of toys;
John plays with string, and John will sing
If ever John makes any noise.

But one room is enough for them.
His mother sews the rich man's clothes,
While John begs in Jerusalem.
(His father died five years ago.)

In the mornings John must rush right out
To sit beside the Temple gate;
He taps his pan and stops each man—
While P. Ben sleeps till very late.

"God bless you, sir," John says to men
Who strut the streets in majesty,
"This rip in your slipper my mother can mend."
P. Ben cries, "Who will wait on *me*?"

John calls to ladies riding high
In coaches pulled by puffing boys:
"I'll work for you; I pull well too!"
"My toys," Ben weeps, "Who took my toys?"

So John is running here and there;
He's pulling coaches, begging clothes,
While Benjamin Methuselah
Has servants come to blow his nose.

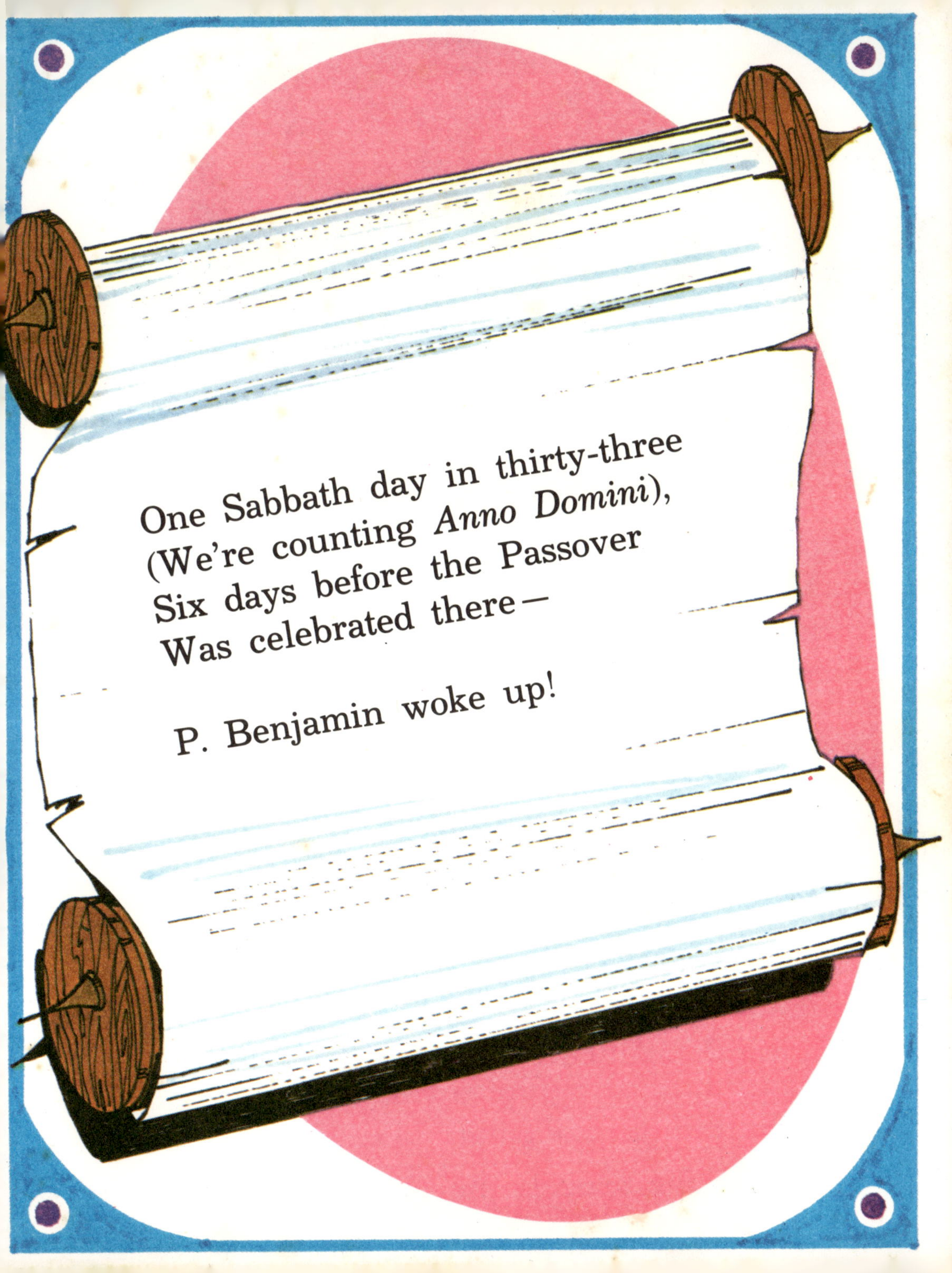
One Sabbath day in thirty-three
(We're counting *Anno Domini*),
Six days before the Passover
Was celebrated there—
P. Benjamin woke up!

“I want my mother here,” he cried
As he was jumping out of bed;
“Get all five servants!” And when they came,
This is the speech that P. Benjamin said:

"It's Sabbath day, and I am good—
I mean I'm *feeling* good today;
So good, in fact, I'm going to give
Exactly seven things away!

"Now, I will pick and choose what goes
Into the Temple treasury:
This, that, not that, not these, but those;
That's seven. Okay, follow me!"

First Benjamin Methuselah
Mounted his sable Arabian horse;
His parents followed riding mares;
The servants marched on foot, of course.

They circled every wealthy hill—
That's seven in Jerusalem—
Till every beggar stood stock still,
And every man had gaped at them.

"I'm going to the Temple now,"
Ben cried, "to give up three plus four;
That's seven, if you folks will add.
Can any boy do any more?"

Can any boy do any more?—
That's what he said; that's what he swore.
Well, John sat at the Temple gate.
And all he owned was what he wore.

P. Benjy spied him sitting there:
"Why, look at him," he said, "so skinny!
I'm feeling *very* good today,
So give that beggar boy a penny."

Ben went inside, swelled up with pride,
And prayed, "O Heaven, look at me!
I'm not like those in beggars' clothes;
I bring these seven things to Thee."

He dropped them in, and what a din!
They sounded like thunder resounding in heaven:
One plunked, two rang, two made a clang,
Two pounded the copperlike drums: that's seven.

And then John's mother came to give
The penny John had given her.
It tinkled in the treasury
No louder than a kitten's purr.

P. Benjamin Methuselah,
He heard this noise and laughed and called,
"One cent! One cent! *I* gave it to them!
Why, that's just nothing, nothing at all!"

"You're wrong, my friend; it's everything."
P. Benjy jumped, surprised: "Who's there?"
"It's Jesus," someone said, "the Lord."
And Benjy cried, "That isn't fair!"

"Fair? Fair?" said Jesus, "Very fair.
You gave God some of many things;
This widow put in *all she had*
And that's not some; it's everything.

"You add it up; see what you get;
What's all plus all? It's close to Heaven.
But one plus two plus two plus two
Is seven, friend; it's only seven."

The Lord kissed John. He touched his mom.
"I love you two," said Christ the Lord.
"You gave Me all you had in store:
Your love, your penny from the poor.
No one could give Me any more."

Dear Parents:

Jesus' commentary about the widow's offering is a short one, but its message comes through loud and clear. She who gave all she had to God gave far more than the rich worshipers who gave just a portion. Does Jesus really mean that we should give all our money and possessions away? Or is He talking about how we should feel about them? Perhaps what He is saying is that we should love God so very much that everything else comes second in importance. If we were called upon to give up all we own we could.

Fictitious P. Benjamin Methuselah was quite committed to his luxurious life. He felt he was doing a great and noble thing by giving God just a little portion of his possessions. In fact he was so puffed up that he reminds us just a little of the Pharisee in the parable of the Pharisee and the Publican.

On the other hand, John and his mother have very little and gladly give even that away, because God is more important to them than *things*. And God, in the person of Jesus, is well pleased with their small gift.

Help your child see the difference in attitude involved. How did P. Benjamin Methuselah feel about his gift? How did he feel about himself for giving it? Why do you think John and his mother gave all the money they had? What did Jesus say about their gift?

Explain to the child that we can give gifts to God in many ways. Jesus tells us one very good way in Matthew 25: by helping others. Perhaps he can think of someone he can help.

The Editor